The HUMAN BODY

Silver Dolphin
San Diego, California

Adventures in SCIENCE
The HUMAN BODY

Silver Dolphin

Silver Dolphin Books
An imprint of Printers Row Publishing Group
10350 Barnes Canyon Road, Suite 100, San Diego, CA 92121
www.silverdolphinbooks.com

© 2017 Silver Dolphin Books

Printers Row Publishing Group is a division of Readerlink Distribution Services, LLC.
Silver Dolphin Books is a registered trademark of Readerlink Distribution Services, LLC.

All notations of errors or omissions should be addressed to Silver Dolphin Books, Editorial Department, at the above address

ISBN: 978-1-68412-129-8

Written by Courtney Acampora
Designed by Creative Giant Inc.

Manufactured, printed, and assembled in Shenzhen, China. First printing, May 2017. HH/05/17.

21 20 19 18 17 1 2 3 4 5

Images copyright Thinkstock

CONTENTS

INTRODUCTION TO
The HUMAN BODY

Bodies come in all shapes and sizes. On the outside, humans look different, but on the inside we're all the same. The human body is made up of skin, bones, blood, and much more. If you dig a little deeper and look under a microscope, you'd see that every part of the human body is made up of **cells**. Cells are the building blocks of every living thing—including you.

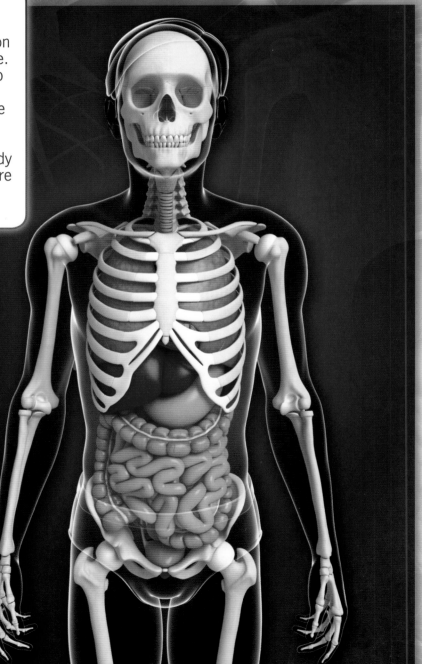

The human body is a mix of cells and systems that work together to do things such as kick goals at a soccer game, paint pictures, solve problems, and even eat birthday cake! Cells group together to form tissue, and tissues combine to make up organs. Organs work together to form a system. Systems help us breathe, move, digest food, and much more.

Let's take a look at the different parts of the human body, explore its systems, and then discover what our bodies need to stay healthy!

CELLS, GENES, and TISSUES

Cells are microscopic, which means you can't see them without a very strong microscope. Some living things are made of just one cell, but humans are made of trillions of cells. Different kinds of cells make up the human body. The human body has 75 trillion cells total, and every single one of them is a living factory that is busy 24 hours a day.

Just as their name suggests, cells are like small rooms. Inside these rooms are tiny parts that the human body needs to stay alive. Humans have more than 200 different kinds of cells, and each kind has a special job to do. Some cells form tissues such as bone, skin, and eyes. Others make important materials such as sweat, saliva, and earwax. Very special cells—sperm in men and eggs in women—only exist to create new humans.

PARTS OF A CELL

- Lysosome
- Nucleus
- Nucleolus
- Mitochondrion
- Golgi apparatus
- Centriole

 Did You Know?

The ostrich egg, which weighs about five pounds, contains the largest cell!

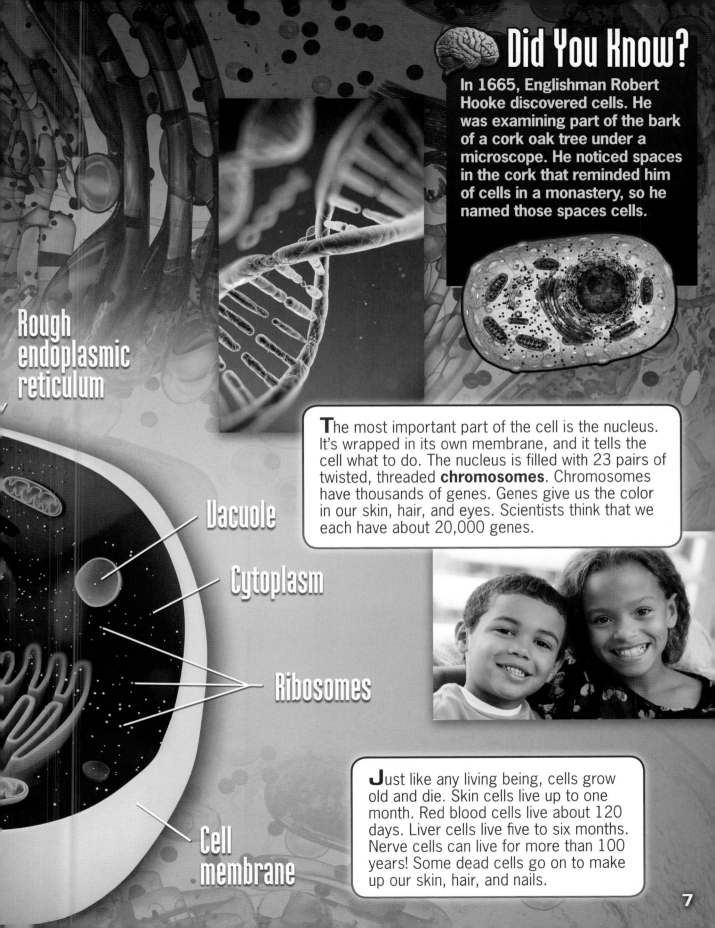

Rough endoplasmic reticulum

Vacuole

Cytoplasm

Ribosomes

Cell membrane

The most important part of the cell is the nucleus. It's wrapped in its own membrane, and it tells the cell what to do. The nucleus is filled with 23 pairs of twisted, threaded **chromosomes**. Chromosomes have thousands of genes. Genes give us the color in our skin, hair, and eyes. Scientists think that we each have about 20,000 genes.

Just like any living being, cells grow old and die. Skin cells live up to one month. Red blood cells live about 120 days. Liver cells live five to six months. Nerve cells can live for more than 100 years! Some dead cells go on to make up our skin, hair, and nails.

7

SKIN, HAIR, and NAILS

It may be hard to believe, but the largest organ of the human body isn't inside you . . . it covers you! Skin is the largest and heaviest organ. It wraps around you and protects your insides.

It keeps harmful elements such as germs and other tiny organisms from getting into your body. Skin keeps blood, water, muscles, tissues, and nerves inside your body, and keeps your body's temperature stable.

Skin is made up of three layers:

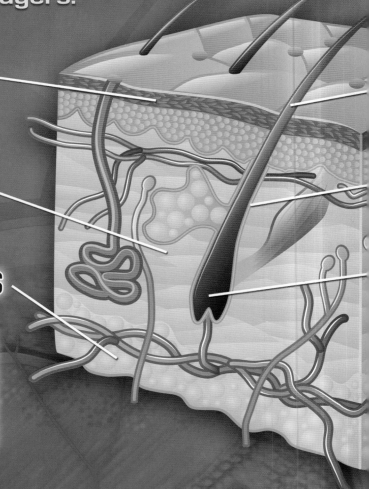

EPIDERMIS

DERMIS

SUBCUTANEOUS

The epidermis is the top, tough layer. It has four layers of cells that die and renew every 28 to 30 days. **Melanin** is a pigment in the epidermis; it determines the darkness of your skin. The more melanin you have, the darker your skin.

The melanin in hair, as in skin, is what makes hair blond, brown, red, or black. Some hair, such as the hair on your head, helps keep the body warm. Eyelashes and eyebrows protect the eyes from bright light. Depending on genetics, the hair on one's head grows an inch every 71 days for up to 10 years.

Our thickest skin is on our feet and our thinnest skin is on our eyelids.

Rod

Follicle

Hair root

Blood vessels

Hair grows from a hair root in a follicle, which is a tiny pit in the skin. New cells grow under the root, forming a rod. The rod is pushed through the skin as cells continue to grow. As the rod grows through skin, it dies and hardens into **keratin**. Keratin is what forms your strands of hair.

Nails are also made of keratin. They have roots, too, and they are also pushed through the skin by the growth of new cells under the roots. Nails grow to protect your fingers and toes. Fingernails also come in handy when you have an itch!

BONES, JOINTS, an

Your skin protects everything inside your body, but the skeleton is what gives your body shape and helps you stand upright. Bones work with muscles so you can move. They are made of calcium and collagen. The calcium gives bones strength, and the central bone marrow helps the body make blood.

As well as giving you shape, bones also have the important job of protecting the soft parts of the body. The skull protects the brain; the ribs form a cage around the heart, lungs, and liver; and the spine surrounds the nerves in the spinal cord.

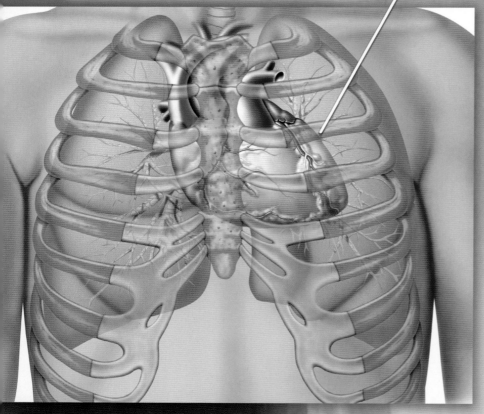

Rib cage

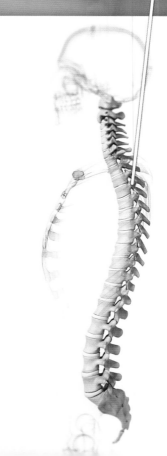

Spinal column

the SKELETON

Human skeleton

- Clavicle
- Sternum
- Humerous
- Vertebrae
- Radius
- Metacarpals (hand bones)
- Femur
- Phalanges (fingers and toes)
- Fibula
- Tibia
- Metatarsals (foot bones)

Humans are born with 300 bones, but, as babies grow, their bones fuse together. Adults have a total of 206 bones.

Skull

- Scapula (shoulder blades)
- Ilium (hip bone)

BONES, JOINTS, and the SKELETON

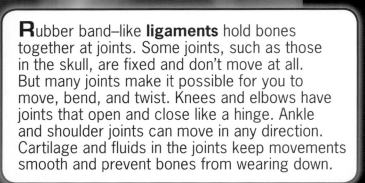

Rubber band–like **ligaments** hold bones together at joints. Some joints, such as those in the skull, are fixed and don't move at all. But many joints make it possible for you to move, bend, and twist. Knees and elbows have joints that open and close like a hinge. Ankle and shoulder joints can move in any direction. Cartilage and fluids in the joints keep movements smooth and prevent bones from wearing down.

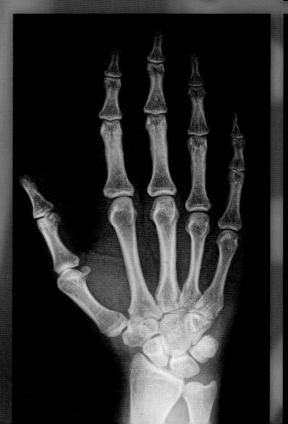

Bones make up our arms, hands, feet, and even ears, where you can find the smallest human bone. Altogether, bones make up the skeleton, the framework of the human body.

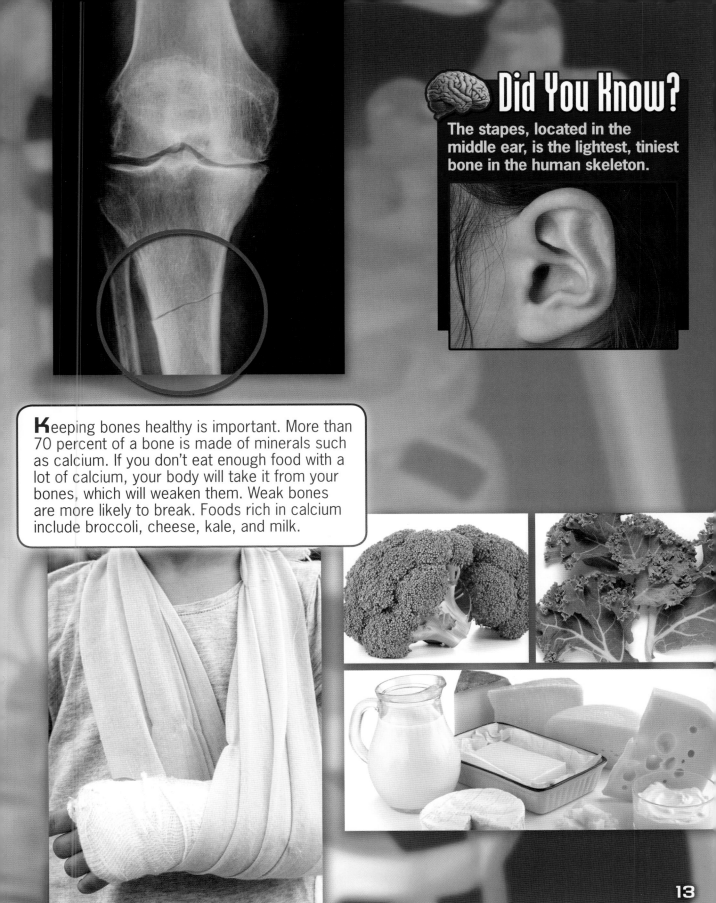

Keeping bones healthy is important. More than 70 percent of a bone is made of minerals such as calcium. If you don't eat enough food with a lot of calcium, your body will take it from your bones, which will weaken them. Weak bones are more likely to break. Foods rich in calcium include broccoli, cheese, kale, and milk.

The FIVE SENSES

A sense is a way to experience the world around you. Each sense is connected to a part of the body. The sense of taste, for instance, lies on your tongue.

TASTE

If you have ever stuck out your tongue in the mirror, you may have noticed little bumps covering your tongue. These are taste buds. Typically, children have more taste buds than adults, with approximately 10,000 taste buds. On average, adults have around 5,000. Your sense of taste doesn't work alone. The way food smells affects how it tastes.

The tongue's basic tastes:

Sour

Bitter

Salty

Unami

Sweet

Taste buds

SMELL

Your nose is used for breathing, but it also picks up all the good and bad smells around you. Tiny hairs in your nose can sense odors. Information from these tiny hairs and taste buds travel to your brain. That's where the smell and taste of the food you're eating combine so you can fully enjoy the flavors of your snack.

Did You Know?

A dog's sense of smell is about a thousand times more sensitive than a human's!

The sense of smell isn't just used for eating, though. It allows you to smell flowers and perfumes, and it warns you of dangers such as fire when you smell smoke.

The FIVE SENSES

SIGHT

We rely on our sense of sight more than any other sense. Your two eyes work together to see what's around you. They are protected by eyebrows, eyelashes, and eyelids. Blinking eyelids keep eyes lubricated, or moist, by spreading tears around.

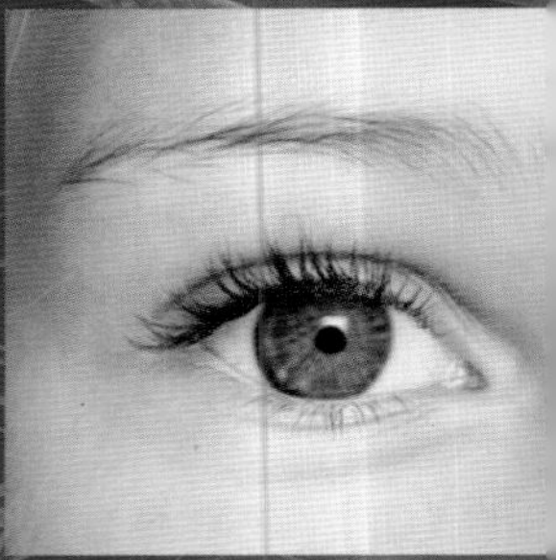

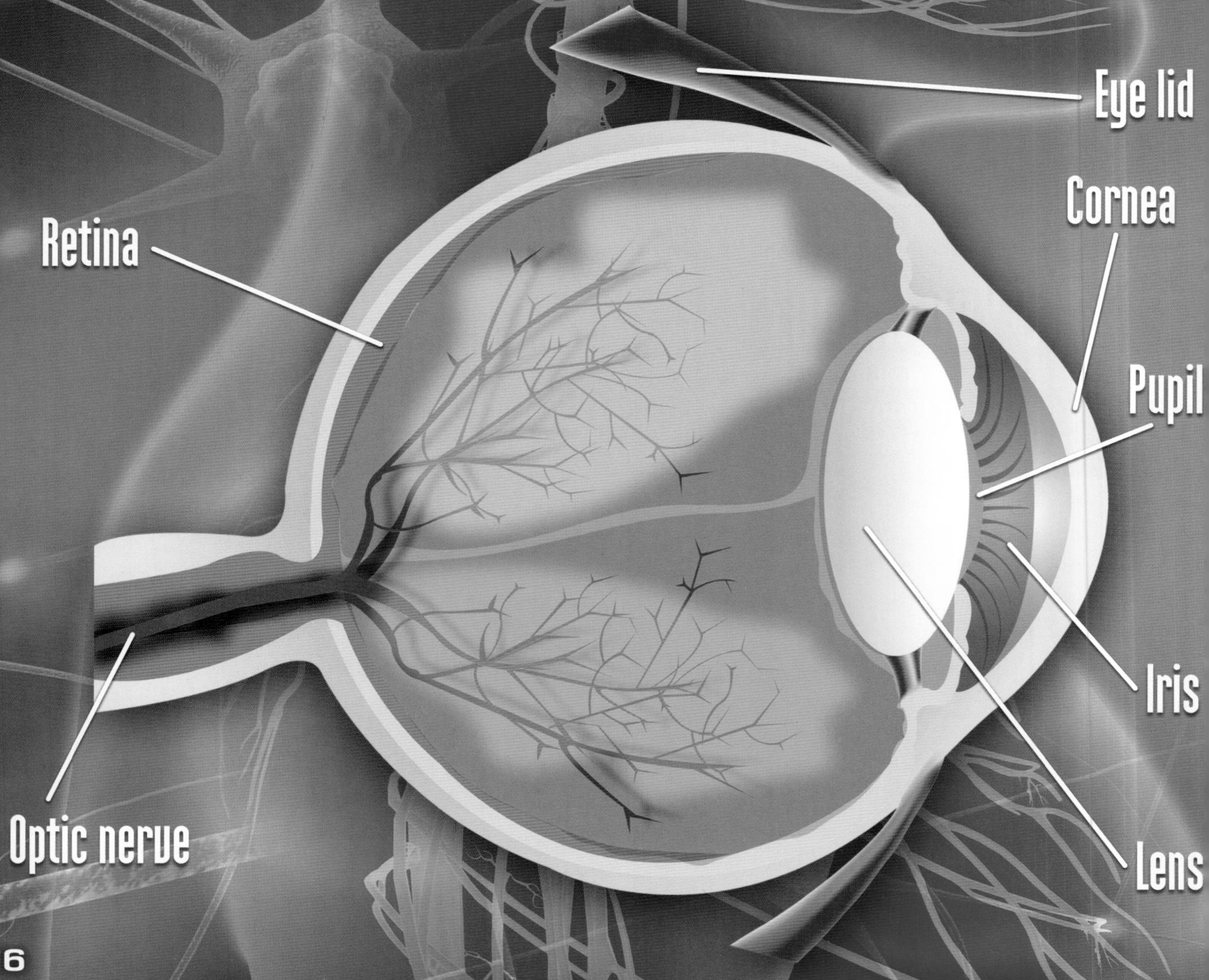

Eye lid

Cornea

Pupil

Retina

Iris

Optic nerve

Lens

HEARING

The ears take sound waves from the air and send them to the brain. Your ears are made up of three parts—outer ear, middle ear, and inner ear. The outer ear is the part you can see. The outer ear catches sound waves and funnels them down the ear canal. Earwax is produced to keep the ear clean of dirt and germs.

Outer ear

Semicircular canals

Cochlea

Ear canal

Cochlear nerve

Did You Know?

Some people are color blind, meaning they cannot see the difference between red and green colors. Do you see a number in the image below?

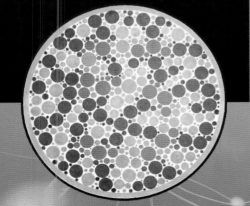

TOUCH

The sense of touch is all over your body, inside and out. But your skin is the major source. When you touch something, neurons produce electrical signals. The signals travel through nerves to your spinal cord, which sends them to your brain.From these signals, the brain can recognize whether you're touching something that is hot or cold, smooth or rough.

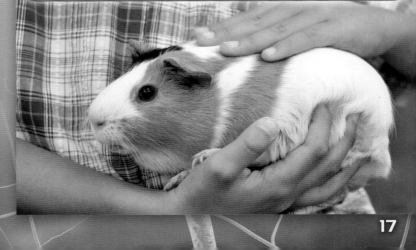

MUSCLES, TENDONS,

Muscles take energy from the food you eat and turn it into power. Muscles help the body move and help us blink our eyes, kick a ball, take a breath, digest food, and much more. They work by contracting (squeezing) and releasing. Some muscles do this without you even thinking about it, but it's up to you to move the other muscles.

The human body has about 650 muscles. They are made of tissues, and there are three types of muscular tissue that help the body with movement:

CARDIAC MUSCLE

SMOOTH MUSCLE

SKELETAL MUSCLE

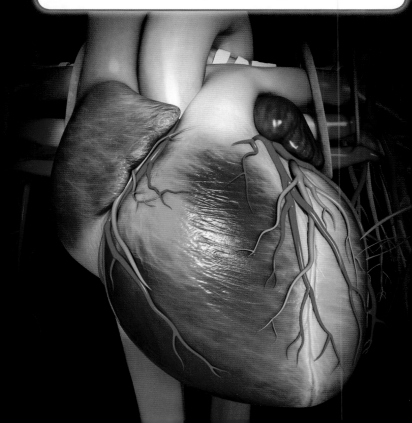

Cardiac means "of the heart." The cardiac muscle squeezes and releases the heart to make it beat and pump blood through your systems. It is a muscle that works automatically without you even thinking about it. And even though the cardiac muscle works nonstop, it doesn't get tired.

and LIGAMENTS

Smooth muscles move automatically. They work in hollow organs such as your stomach, where smooth muscles help push food through your body.

Muscular system

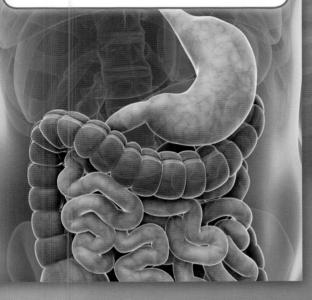

Skeletal muscles are connected to your bones. They form your shape, and you have to think about moving skeletal muscles. Nerves inside a muscle get messages from your brain to move. Skeletal muscles help you walk, play, lift, and more.

You can make skeletal muscles bigger by making them work. When you lift weights or do sit-ups, you're causing tiny tears. As the muscles repair themselves, they're building themselves up.

MUSCLES, TENDONS, and LIGAMENTS

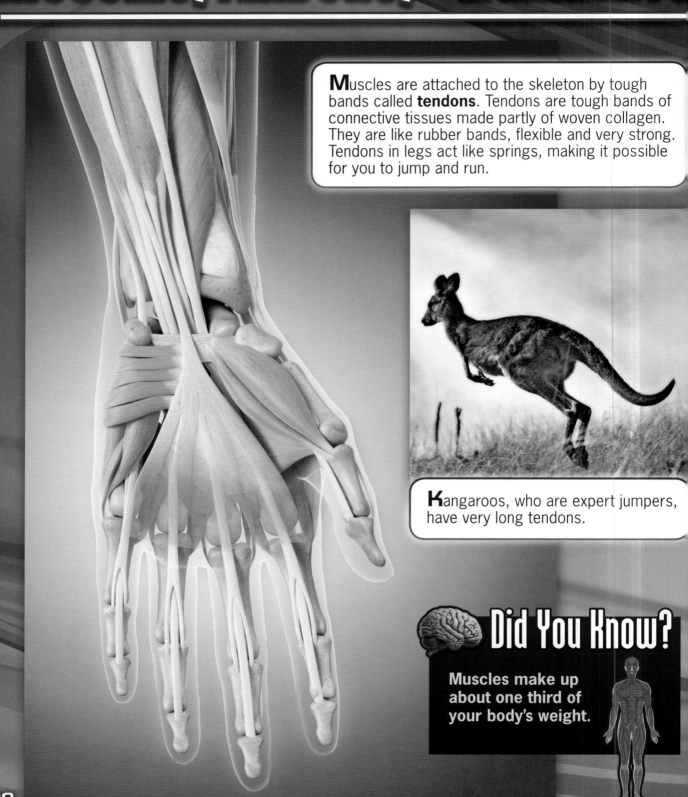

Muscles are attached to the skeleton by tough bands called **tendons**. Tendons are tough bands of connective tissues made partly of woven collagen. They are like rubber bands, flexible and very strong. Tendons in legs act like springs, making it possible for you to jump and run.

Kangaroos, who are expert jumpers, have very long tendons.

Did You Know?

Muscles make up about one third of your body's weight.

Like tendons, ligaments are connective tissues. Instead of connecting muscle to bone, ligaments connect bone to bone at joints. Unlike tendons, ligaments don't help the body move, but rather hold things together. They limit joint movement and help keep the human body stable.

Although tendons and ligaments are both flexible, only ligaments are elastic. Stretching ligaments is how dancers and gymnasts are able to do the splits. People who are double-jointed can thank their very flexible ligaments.

The BRAIN

Everything you feel, think, do, and dream has to go through your brain.

It's no wonder that the brain is well protected. This wrinkly, three-pound command center for the human body sits atop the spinal cord and is surrounded by a hard, bony skull. The brain has billions of tiny nerve cells called **neurons** that connect to other neurons by tiny branches. Electrical and chemical messages from neurons zip around your body through your nervous system at 150 miles per hour. Your brain works faster than a computer!

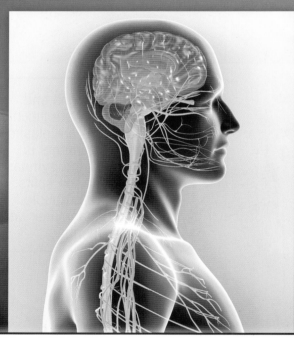

 Did You Know?

Have you ever wondered why you can't tickle yourself? It has to do with the brain's self-awareness. The cerebellum predicts sensations before a particular movement. If the brain knows what's about to happen, it cuts off the response caused by a tickle!

Messages travel to parts of your body through the nerves in the spine. Sensory nerves collect information about what you see, feel, hear, smell, and taste, then send it to the brain for interpretation. Motor nerves communicate your brain's orders to other parts of the body.

The brain has three main sections:

CEREBRUM

The cerebrum is the main part of the brain, and the largest. It controls thoughts, speech, and the senses. When you're at school or doing homework, you're using your cerebrum. It also holds all your memories and controls muscles such as those in your legs and arms.

CEREBELLUM

The cerebellum is in the back of your skull behind the brain stem. It controls balance and posture. It also coordinates movement so you can walk, turn around, and do things such as tie your shoes and play video games.

BRAIN STEM

The brain stem connects the brain to the spinal cord to form the central nervous system. It has the important jobs of keeping your heart beating, blood circulating, and your stomach processing food. It does all this and more automatically!

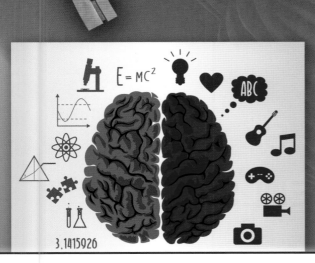

$E = MC^2$

ABC

3.1415926

 # Did You Know?

Children as young as four days old can distinguish the vowel sounds of the language they hear every day from those of a foreign language.

A groove in the middle of the cerebrum divides it in half. The right half of the cerebrum controls the left side of your body, and the left half of the cerebrum controls the right side of your body. Scientists believe that the right side of the cerebrum is the more creative half and deals with things such as art and music. The left half figures things out and controls speech.

The HEART and BLOOD

The human body needs blood to stay alive, and the heart makes sure blood gets to every part of the body—very quickly. It takes just one minute for blood from the heart to reach each cell in the body. Blood flows through tubes called blood vessels. Together, the heart and blood vessels make up the cardiovascular system.

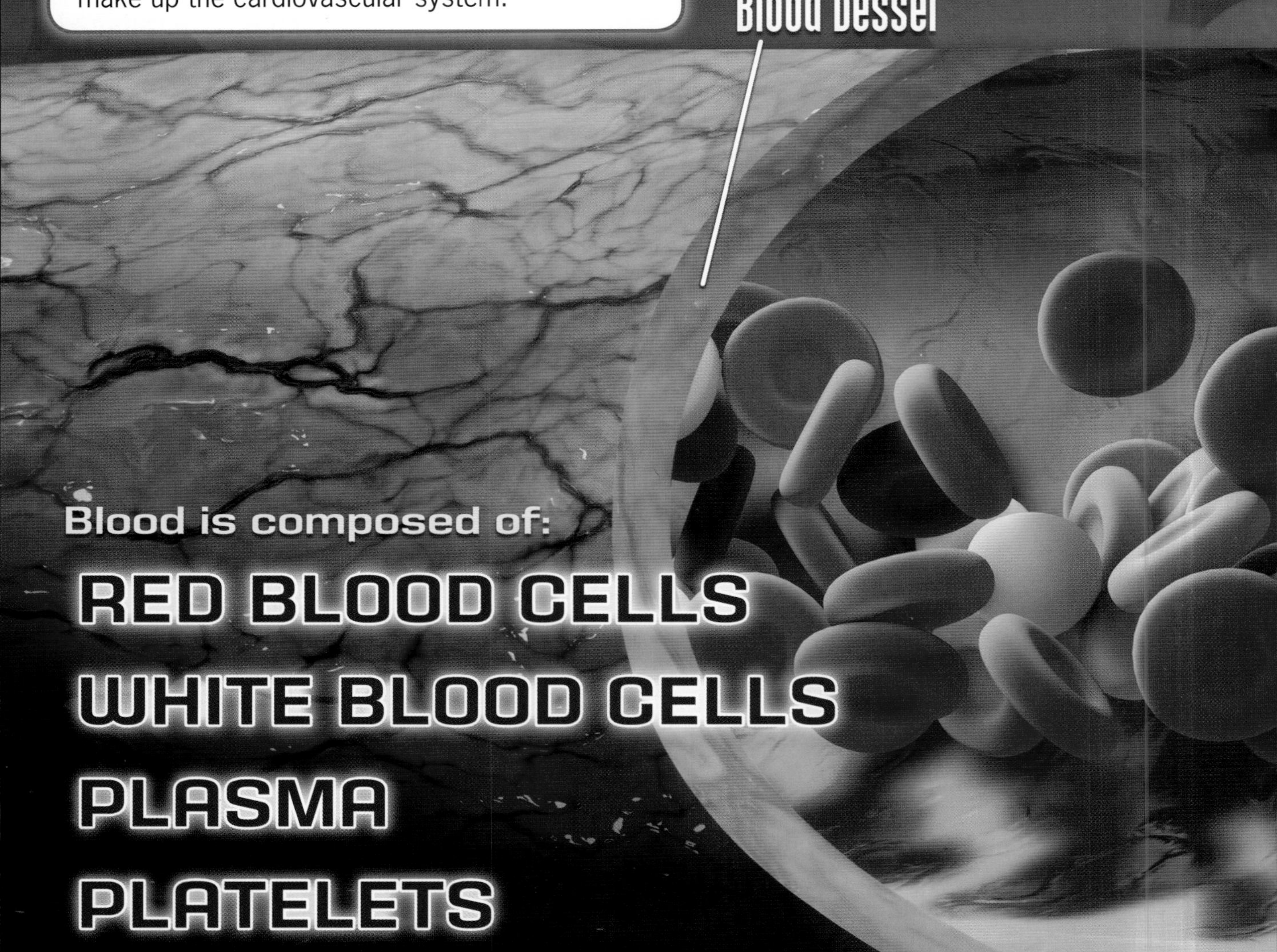

Blood vessel

Blood is composed of:

RED BLOOD CELLS

WHITE BLOOD CELLS

PLASMA

PLATELETS

Red blood cells are born in bone marrow. Once in the bloodstream, red blood cells deliver oxygen from the lungs to the rest of the body. They also take carbon dioxide from the body to the lungs to be breathed out of the body. The most important job for white blood cells is to fight infections.

Plasma

White blood cell

Red blood cell

Platelet

Plasma is the watery part of blood. It moves blood cells, nutrients, waste, and more through the body. Platelets are cells that help blood clot. Clotting is what blood does to stop bleeding.

The HEART and BLOOD

The heart is a muscle located in the middle of the chest, protected by the ribs. The heart's beating and pumping circulates blood through your body.

The heart is made up of four chambers:

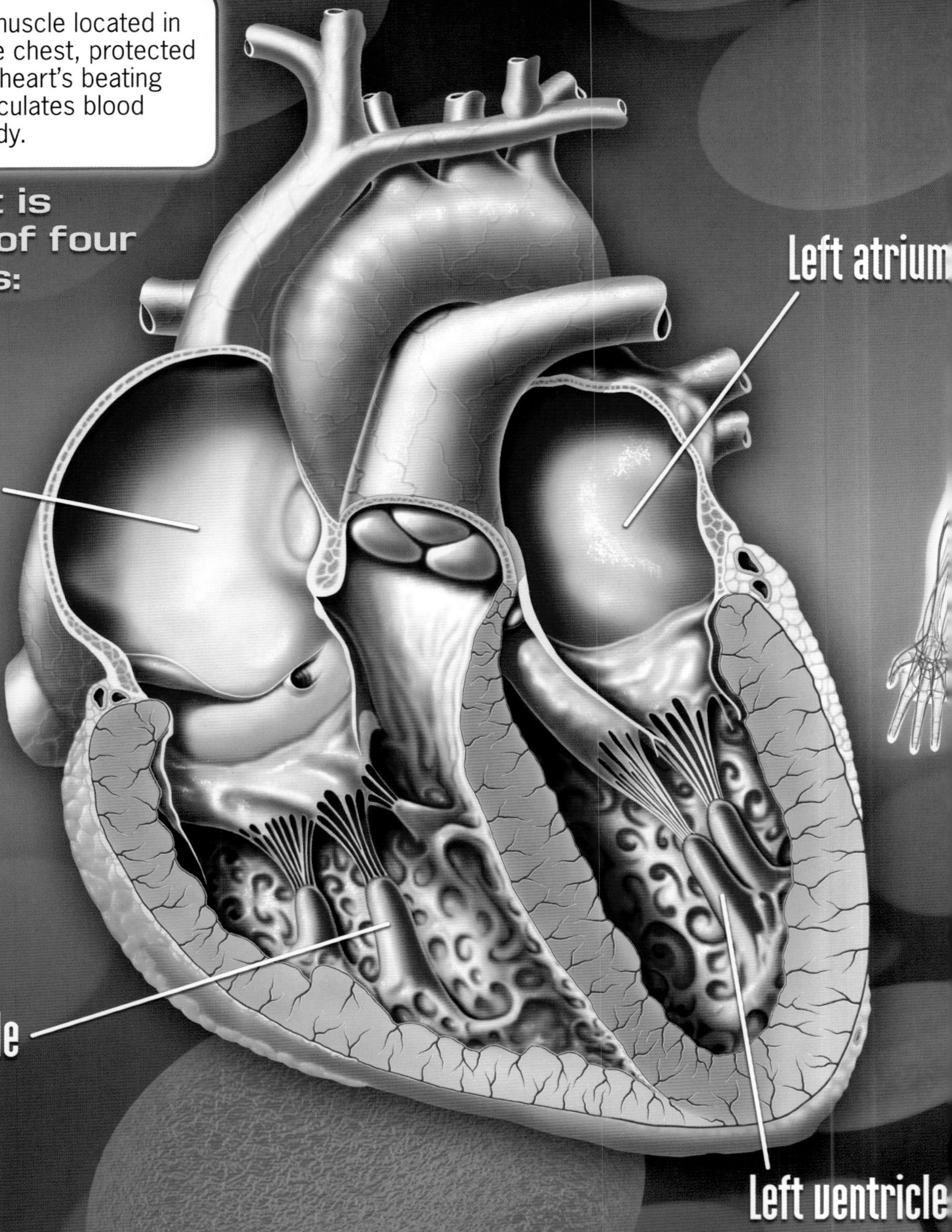

Right atrium

Left atrium

Right ventricle

Left ventricle

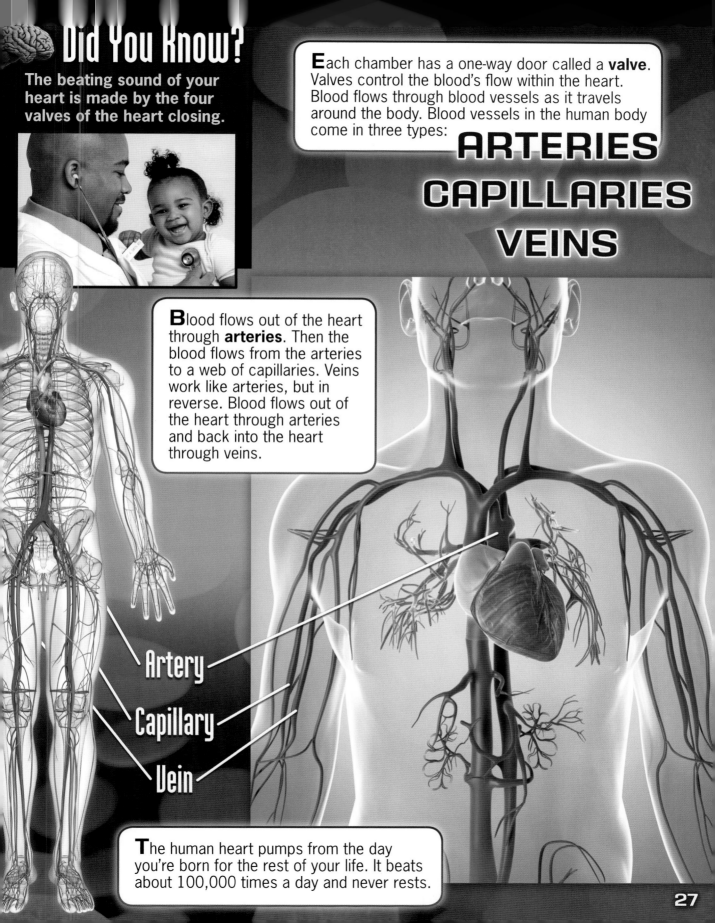

Did You Know?

The beating sound of your heart is made by the four valves of the heart closing.

Each chamber has a one-way door called a **valve**. Valves control the blood's flow within the heart. Blood flows through blood vessels as it travels around the body. Blood vessels in the human body come in three types:

ARTERIES
CAPILLARIES
VEINS

Blood flows out of the heart through **arteries**. Then the blood flows from the arteries to a web of capillaries. Veins work like arteries, but in reverse. Blood flows out of the heart through arteries and back into the heart through veins.

Artery

Capillary

Vein

The human heart pumps from the day you're born for the rest of your life. It beats about 100,000 times a day and never rests.

The LUNGS

Your lungs fill with air every time you take a breath. When you breathe in, you're filling your lungs with oxygen.

Oxygen is a gas that is in the air, and the human body needs it to stay alive. You have two lungs in your body, protected by your ribs. The left lung is a bit smaller than the right lung to make room for the heart.

Lungs are the major organs of the respiratory system. When you inhale, the air flows down your windpipe, through one of two tubes, and into each of your lungs. These tubes branch into even smaller tubes called bronchioles.

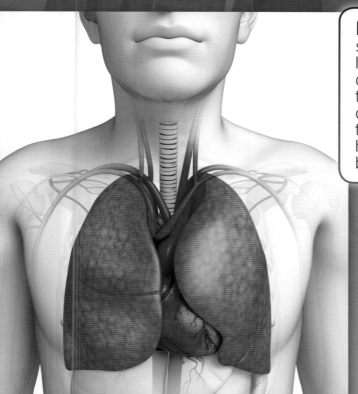

At the tips of the bronchioles are clumps of sacs called alveoli. The 600 million alveoli in the lungs fill with air with each breath. The alveoli connect to the heart and oxygen seeps through the alveoli's thin walls and into the blood-filled capillaries. The now oxygen-rich blood flows through blood vessels and into the heart. The heart pumps blood throughout the body and brings oxygen and nutrients to the body's tissues.

Did You Know?

No matter how hard we exhale, our lungs will always retain air. This makes the lungs the only human organs that can float on water.

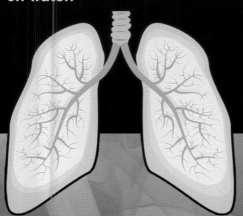

Lungs have another important task—they help you talk! When you exhale, lungs push air up the windpipe and voice box to your vocal cords. Air makes the vocal cords vibrate, which is how you make sounds to speak.

IMMUNE SYSTEM

When you're sick, you may notice that your lymph nodes (glands in your neck) are sore. This means your lymphatic system is busy at work! This is an important system that prevents you from getting sick and helps fight infections.

Like the cardiovascular system, the lymphatic system is made up of vessels. Instead of blood flowing through them, these vessels are full of lymph. Lymph is a colorless fluid, similar to plasma, that contains a lot of white blood cells.

White blood cells

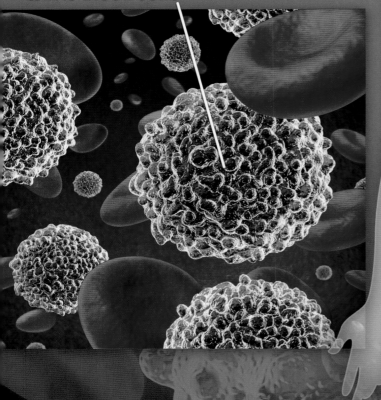

Lymphatic system

Lymph nodes

Lymph nodes work as germ filters and are scattered all throughout your body. As the lymph passes through the nodes, they filter out germs. Each node is also full of lymphocytes. When they get a message about a germ inside the body, the lymphocytes quickly get to work multiplying and making the antibodies take care of it. Nodes near the site of the infection may swell and become sore.

Did You Know?

Allergies affect nearly 30 percent of adults and 40 percent of children.

Sometimes the body overreacts to things that are normally harmless—things such as peanuts, pollen, or cat hair. These result in allergies. Often when a person experiences allergies, they will have the same symptoms as when their body is fighting a cold—a sore throat, sneezing, and stuffed nose.

STOMACH and DIGESTION

The stomach is where food is stored. It is a muscular sac that is shaped like a bean. It is located slightly on your left beneath your lower ribs.

Your body digests stored food slowly, over four to six hours. The stomach is the reason you can eat a large meal every few hours instead of eating frequently throughout the day. Because it stores food, the stomach is the widest section of the digestive system. Digestion is the process of breaking down food so it can be used to fuel the body.

Esophagus

Liver

Gallbladder

Pancreas

Spleen

Stomach

Small intestine

Large intestine

Appendix

1. Believe it or not, digestion actually begins in the brain! When you're hungry, if you just think about food or smell food, your brain sends signals for your mouth to water. The water is called saliva.

2. Saliva turns food into a gooey liquid so the body can use the nutrients. Chemicals in saliva start breaking down the food. When you swallow it, the food flows down the throat through the esophagus.

3. The esophagus leads to the stomach where stomach acid works with stomach muscles to break down the food into smaller, soggier pieces. The pancreas is a gland behind the stomach. Fluids from the pancreas help digest fats and proteins. Bile, a liquid from the liver, helps fat get absorbed by the bloodstream. And the gallbladder stores fat until it's needed by the body.

4. Then the food enters the small intestines where it can spend hours being digested. The small intestine fills with a nutritious blend of protein, minerals, and vitamins. Then, with the help of millions of tiny nubs called villi, this healthful mix passes through the small intestine and enters the bloodstream.

5. From the bloodstream, the nutrients go to the liver to be stored or sent into the body as needed. The liver also sends waste, the parts the body can't use, on to the large intestine.

6. At about four inches around, the large intestine is twice as big as the small intestine, but it's much shorter. When it's stretched out, the small intestine is about twenty feet long. The large intestine, when stretched out, is only five feet long. The large intestine takes the last bit of nutrients from undigested food before passing everything else to become waste.

Did You Know?

Your digestive system is one tube that is about 30 feet long. That's almost as long as a school bus!

GETTING RID of WASTE

What comes in must come out, right? This is true of the human body.

Every breath you let out gets rid of waste. In this case, the waste is **carbon dioxide**. You also get rid of waste from eating and drinking—your body uses what it needs and gets rid of the rest.

Lungs

Kidneys

Ureters

Bladder

Two kidneys rest right under your ribs. As blood flows through the body, it passes through the kidneys. Kidneys filter out the leftovers that the body doesn't need. If this waste were to build up in your body, you'd become sick. The kidneys need water to help move waste along. Waste materials and extra water filter out of the kidneys, down the ureters, and into the bladder—ready to come out as urine.

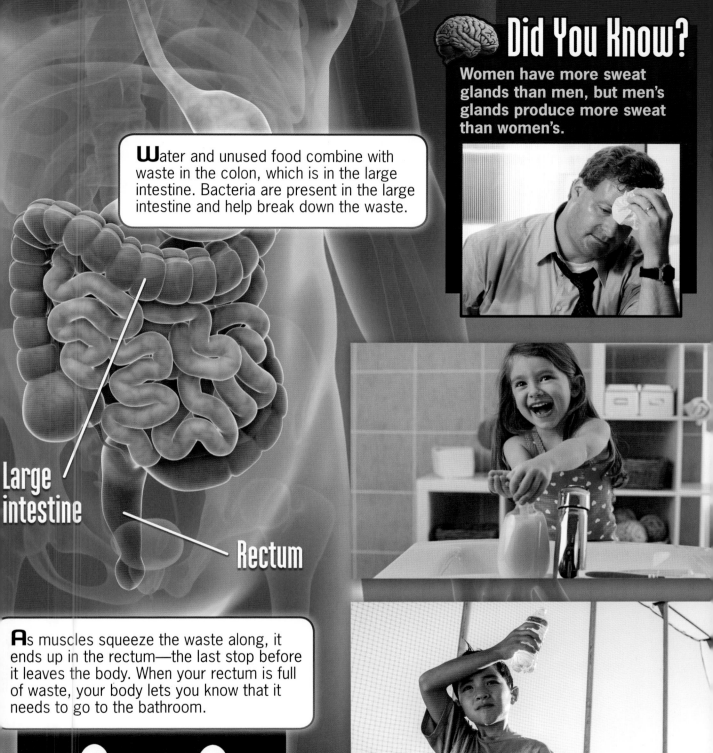

Women have more sweat glands than men, but men's glands produce more sweat than women's.

Water and unused food combine with waste in the colon, which is in the large intestine. Bacteria are present in the large intestine and help break down the waste.

Large intestine

Rectum

As muscles squeeze the waste along, it ends up in the rectum—the last stop before it leaves the body. When your rectum is full of waste, your body lets you know that it needs to go to the bathroom.

Other forms of waste in the human body include earwax, mucus, and sweat.

EXERCISE and KEEPING HEALTHY

The human body is an extraordinary system that works together to ensure everything works properly. However, exercise and nutrition are important things we must do to keep the body in tip-top shape.

Staying active and fit keeps your muscles strong—even your heart muscle. Exercise makes you flexible and makes it easier to breathe. It even puts you in a good mood! When you exercise, your brain actually releases a chemical that makes you happy. Exercise is fun, too! Jogging, swimming, riding a bike, playing basketball or football are all forms of exercise.

NUTRITION

Paired with exercise, nutrition is also important to feed your body the nutrients and vitamins it needs.

Carbohydrates

These are your body's main source of energy. Carbohydrates are sugars that are easy for the body to convert to energy. Bread, rice, grains, pasta, and potatoes contain carbohydrates.

Protein

Protein is important for your body's growth and repair. It is used to grow muscle, build hair and nails, and repair skin. Meat, fish, beans, and dairy products all have protein.

Fat

In the right amounts, fat is an important part of your diet. It helps the body use vitamins and keeps nerves and cells healthy. Cheese, butter, oil, and nuts all contain fat.

Vitamins

Vitamins, along with minerals, are important for keeping the body working properly. Vitamins make bones, help your body heal, and help fight off germs. Most foods have a variety of different types of vitamins.

Did You Know?

If you break a bone or get a scrape, Vitamin C gets to work to help you heal properly.

The human body is an amazing machine with extraordinary systems that work together to allow us to live healthy and happy lives. Next time you're playing your favorite sport or eating a yummy snack, think about all the intricate and phenomenal body parts that are busily working—without you even thinking about it!

GLOSSARY

Arteries: vessels that transport oxygenated blood from the heart to the tissues of the body

Carbon dioxide: colorless gas that is vital to life on Earth. It is produced when people breathe out and is absorbed by plants

Cells: tiny building blocks that form living things

Chromosomes: threadlike part of a cell that carries genes

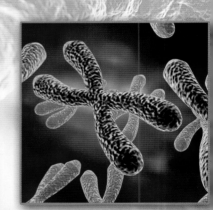

Keratin: protein in hair and nails

Ligaments: bands that hold bones together at the joints

Melanin: substance in the human body that gives color to skin, hair, and eyes

Neurons: cells that receive and send signals within the body

Plasma: liquid part of blood

Platelets: tiny blood cells that clump together to stop bleeding

Tendons: tissue that attaches muscle to other body parts

Value: parts of the heart that make sure blood flows in and out of the heart

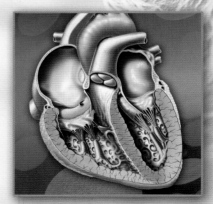

SKELETON MODEL INSTRUCTIONS

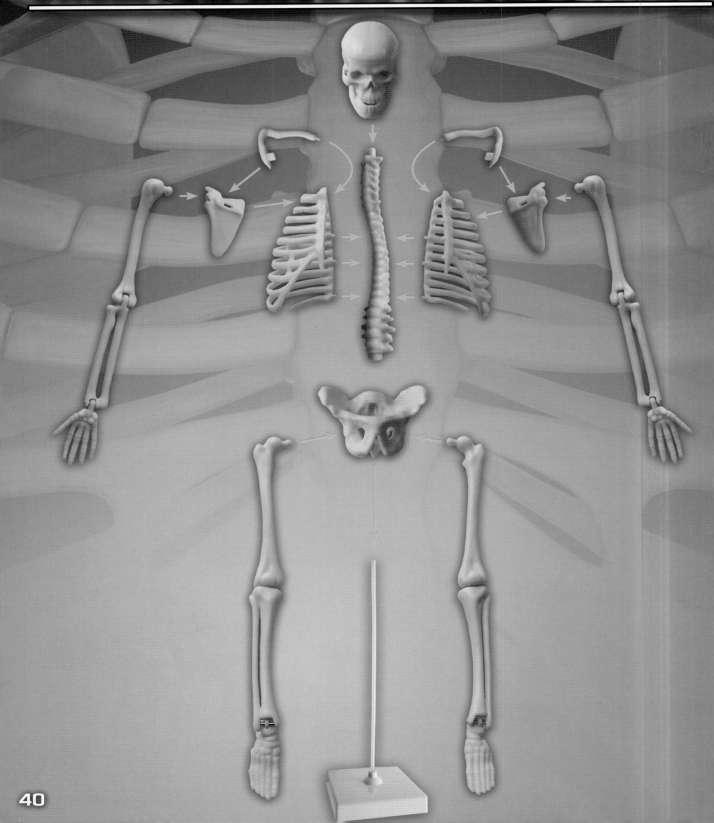